IMAGES
of America

LORAIN COUNTY METRO PARKS

THE FIRST 50 YEARS

Few people have partnered with the Lorain County Metro Parks like Otto Schoepfle. He was equally talented in both business and horticulture. By mixing both of these, he was able to create an amazing formal garden and the means for funding its maintenance and future growth. Schoepfle passed away in 1992, but his garden and his trust will live forever. He is seen here with his beloved cannas.

On the cover: A giant sheer wall of shale corrals a rather placid and shallow stream called the Vermilion River. Despite appearances, however, the Vermilion River does not belong to the cliff, but the cliff belongs to it. Over the course of the last 12,000 years, the river carved this great cliff, and perhaps unwarily, also carved out the perfect valley to host both a fledgling park district and visitors who love to skip flat, black stones. (Courtesy of Lorain County Metro Parks.)

IMAGES
of America

LORAIN COUNTY METRO PARKS

THE FIRST 50 YEARS

Gary S. Gerrone

ARCADIA
PUBLISHING

For all general information contact Arcadia Publishing at:
Telephone 843-853-2070
Fax 843-853-0044
E-mail sales@arcadiapublishing.com
For customer service and orders:
Toll-Free 1-888-313-2665

Visit us on the Internet at www.arcadiapublishing.com

*This book is dedicated to the ladies and gentlemen whose well-focused
vision clearly peered into our future and protected our past.*

CONTENTS

ACKNOWLEDGMENTS

College sociology taught me that agencies, like metro parks, do not actually exist. The foundation of this thinking is that you cannot touch, or talk to, some singular, and unique, entity that is the metro parks. The metro parks are, thank goodness, everywhere, and no one person, place, or thing can individually represent the whole.

There is a whole, however, but it is not tangible; but you do feel it. You do not, however, feel it with your hand, but with the passion of your heart.

It was a firm passion that started the park district, and I thank the many ladies and gentlemen who lit and passed on this wonderful torch. Of these founders, I must single out the late Richard McGinnis. I also thank his wife, Lila, for sharing his vision with as much vigor as if it had happened just this morning.

Bob Hartle inspired me on my first day and still does today. I am indebted to him for his gracious sharing of stories and photographs (but not his secret fishing holes).

Perry F. Johnson was the best professor I ever had. He made "old school" cool, and he diligently erased my overwhelming lack of nature knowledge.

Christie Vargo and Carl Crapo took a chance on hiring me. Their trust in my talents has led me down an incredible trail.

I am appreciative to the current board of park commissioners—Kirk Stewart, Sherrill "Cookie" McLoda, and Stanley Pijor—for allowing me to employ what I enjoy.

I thank Becky Voit and Sylvia Schmitt for their help, support, and understanding, and Joani Longbrake for fixing my grammar.

Dan Martin allowed me this wonderful task of reliving the life of the Lorain County Metro Parks. This was an awesome honor, and I hope that I have done some level of justice to the history of this great organization.

I send countless thanks to the Friends of Metro Parks, as well as all of the park visitors with whom I have had the pleasure of sharing the trail.

My thanks to the staff of Arcadia Publishing, especially Melissa Basilone for her confidence and positive comments.

To my family—I love you and owe you big time.

INTRODUCTION

It was most likely assumed that "county metropolitan park districts" would fill the void between the wild nature of state and national parks and the high recreation of city parks. Although most leaned slightly more toward the former, they fill the gap admirably. But unlike either, metro parks were innately more flexible and more able to evolve to meet the ever-changing needs of the local citizens who directly supported them.

In the beginning, the Lorain County Metro Parks were no different. Its iconic arrowhead logo spoke of what people knew, and expected, from nature parks. Even though most parks were small, they still held within their borders the best of a county's natural and cultural history and, more importantly, what locals considered to be near and dear.

But in the early days, passion and enthusiasm were the dollars and cents of the Lorain County Metro Parks. Free land certainly did not equate to free parks. With Richard McGinnis still pushing the momentum, probate court judge Harold Ewing placing faith, and Henry Minert practicing creative management, they were able to turn Grace Annie Dorothy Bacon DeMuth's free land into an almost free park.

The citizens of Lorain County loved it, and they still do.

The almost corny attributes of Mill Hollow in the early 1960s—such as the geodesic picnic shelter and the wild animal collection—turn out to be nothing more than predictors of the future. Who today could say that the wild-nautilus shape of the French Creek Nature Center or the enclosures of the Carlisle Raptor Center are really any different? Or any less cherished?

In 1961, before the passage of the park district's first levy, the park board put before the citizens a plan to secure parkland within seven miles of every corner of the county. It was an impressive, and seemingly impossible, plan. Still the levy passed, and steps toward this goal were initiated.

By 1980, many parts of the plan were completed. Seven parks, featuring over 4,000 acres, were secured and opened. But the park district still found itself at a strange crossroads. The price of land was ever increasing, and the old retrofitted facilities were far behind the times—and any plans for a Lake Carlisle Reservation had completely dried up! By this time, the animal cages were gone, the camping was gone, and most park reservations equally catered to picnickers and short-term hikers.

It was time for a change. It was time for the Carlisle Visitor Center (CVC).

The CVC did more than provide new and modern facilities for staff and visitors—not the least of which was flush toilets—it created space for the expansion of dreams.

Large indoor spaces led staff and visitors alike to dream. Halloween Walks doubled and diversified yearly. Perry Johnson's passion for bird feeding grew into the addition called the Wildlife Observation Area. Appreciative use of the facility by outside groups also grew. While the 1980s may be seen as a conservative time in the history of the Lorain County Metro Parks, it was nothing of the sort.

Before the end of the decade, the metro parks found themselves securing a new levy and following through with expected promises. At the top of the list was a promise to bring the metro parks to the people. The vector to do this was the 17,000-square-foot French Creek Nature Center (FCNC). Its shape, and initial color scheme, made this facility look as far out as a geodesic dome shelter or the inflatable dam that was to have flooded out the Carlisle Reservation. It was asked many times, "Who came up with such a plan?"

Perhaps the real answer is the forefathers. Well maybe not Richard (Dick) McGinnis, Harold S. Ewing, and Henry L. Minert personally, but it is not without validity that they saw something like this coming, something different, something unusual, something beyond the icon of the arrowhead, and something quite successful. To date, the FCNC has done nothing but add positive evolution to what a metropolitan park district is.

In 1992, an outsider arrived. Like Dick McGinnis, James Daniel Martin had been out there, and he had seen the other side. His past experience with Ohio State Parks and with city parks and recreation in Columbus made him, no doubt, the perfect hybrid to steer a metro park. And like McGinnis, he saw something in Lorain County and its "little park district out in the country." (It has been rumored that he once met Henry Minert as a child.)

Fate notwithstanding, Martin worked the staff, worked the money, and worked the plan. In short time, the Black River Reservation stretched a wild, wonderful, and a very paved, trail between the metropolitan areas of Lorain and Elyria. People could now walk between the largest two cities in the county, and through a metro park no less. Is this not what metropolitan park districts are supposed to do? Is not a high-tech pair of in-line skates screaming past a pair of reminiscing "River Rats" as they pass over a 1,000-foot bridge that crosses the Black River twice within its span pretty darn equal to a geodesic dome shelter reflecting a starkly nautilus-shaped nature center? Was not the overall concept of the 1961 plan for proposed park reservations all about having parkland, as well as services and facilities, close to the public?

In 2007, the Lorain County Metro Parks boasts 24 park reservations. This not only puts a park within an easy seven-mile reach of every citizen, it puts a park into every major community and many areas in between. It would seem that this is an extraordinary accomplishment, and one well beyond the original vision.

But the 1961 plan was designed to take a "paper" park district and give it vision for the future. Like the park district, it has evolved. Subsequent plans, for example, showed the need for such park areas as Sandy Ridge Reservation as early as 1970. But did the plans, or the planners, see SplashZone anywhere on the radar or the financial and conservational stewardship of the wetland mitigation process? Perhaps not, but remember, they opened up the first park one year early by straightening nails and turning utility cable spools into picnic tables. Could there be any better examples that they saw something where others did not?

One

A LITTLE BIT OF HISTORY

This image shows the Great Nest of Brownhelm. This giant bald eagle nest was occupied and added on to for at least 35 consecutive years. Just prior to its demise in 1925, the nest measured 12 feet tall and 8.5 feet wide. It was estimated to have weighed nearly two tons. Eagles were then common to this part of Ohio, and this active nest was studied at great length by Dr. Francis H. Herrick. Note the high angle of the photograph. It was taken from a rickety tower built nearby. Herrick's findings were published in 1929 in *National Geographic* magazine. For the first time, the American public was able to learn in fact and detail of their national emblem. This nest, by all known accounts, still stands as the largest bird tree nest ever found. In recognition of this local natural wonder, the metro parks is fabricating a ground-level replica of this nest at the Carlisle Raptor Center. It is scheduled for unveiling on March 10, 2007—the 87th anniversary of the collapse of the actual Great Nest of Brownhelm.

For most of its length, the Vermilion River flows through a half-mile-wide gorge that is carved over 100 feet into the Cleveland shale that underlies all of Lorain County. It took the river over 7,500 years to do this erosive work. Besides the Cleveland shale, the cliff contains a soft reddish shale near the top. Heavy rain will dissolve this shale and paint the cliffs with a vermilion color.

This stone may look like a turtle, but it is not; nor is it a turtle fossil. Formed through the strange and complicated geologic process of concretion, this septerian concretion is a very local, but very common, find in the Vermilion River valley. Typically two to three inches across, these stones erode out of the Cleveland shale and into the working waters of the Vermilion River.

On the hillside above the Vermilion River Reservation's Bacon Woods Trail is a simple jumble of broken sandstone blocks. One half mile across the valley, another jumble is found. Could these have been connected? They probably were, and they probably formed an amazing natural bridge. Thousands of years of erosion have washed away the support and remnants of this natural wonder. Now only a pair of bookend outcrops remains.

Large pockets of sandstone are found throughout the county. The quality and accessibility of this natural resource initiated many quarrying operations in the mid-1800s. Cleveland Quarries in South Amherst led the way to Lorain County being justifiably known as the sandstone capital of the world. The quarry pictured is within the Indian Hollow Reservation. A hike at this park will likely reveal many clues to its industrial past.

While woolly mammoths once called Lorain County home, their close relative, the American mastodon, was apparently more common. This incredible skull was dug up in the late 1800s in Brownhelm Township. Shown here at the district's 2001 World of the Mammoth exhibit, this skull is now on permanent display at the Carlisle Visitor Center (CVC). The leg bone shown with it was later determined to be that of a modern horse.

The Wisconsin Glacier left a giant basin as a natural northern border of Lorain County. Eventually this basin would become known as Lake Erie, but before it there were several predecessor lakes, and each of these left signature beach ridges. Today's Lake Erie is the shallowest, and southernmost, of the Great Lakes. It is well known as the walleye capital of the world. This view is from Lakeview Park in the city of Lorain.

The knowledge of local American Indian history is dominated by the Late Woodland people. Living in the area over 500 years ago, these resourceful natives farmed, fished, and built defendable settlements. Their clay pots bore very diagnostic markings. The study of these markings has shown that the original residents of Lorain County were the people of the Sandusky Tradition. Pictured here is an unusual find called the weeping shell pendant.

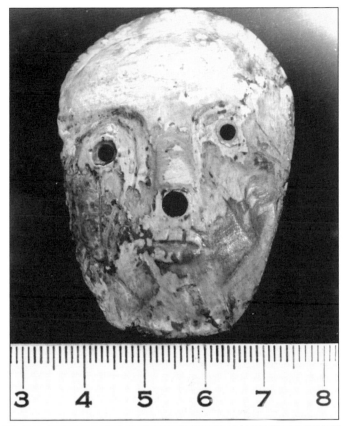

This image shows Brownhelm Mills around 1876. The large structure at left is the mill; the house that Benjamin Bacon built is peaking through trees just right of center. Although not the first to arrive, Bacon became this settlement's most prominent citizen. He purchased the mill in 1835 and built his impressive Greek Revival home in 1845. His heir, Dorothy DeMuth Bacon, donated this property as the first metro park.

This 1950 aerial photograph shows the main branch of the Black River, from just south of the State Route 254 bridge in Sheffield to just north of East Thirty-first Street in Lorain. Besides the fact that this park proposal predates the formation of the Lorain County Metro Park District, there are two other interesting aspects to it. First this view shows, in nearly perfect entirety, the

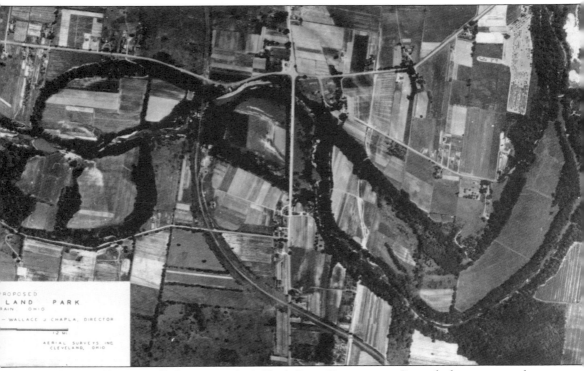

PROPOSED
LAND   PARK
RAIN   OHIO

— WALLACE J CHAPLA, DIRECTOR

1 2 Mi

AERIAL SURVEYS INC
CLEVELAND, OHIO

area that would eventually become today's Black River Reservation. Second, the name on the legend for director of the Department of Public Service is Wallace J. Chapla—a man who would be highly involved with the formation, and formative years, of the Lorain County Metro Parks.

When land is acquired by the metro parks, it often comes with some of the remnants of its past use. Here the mangled metal and brick remains of a sugar shack—a maple sap processing station—tells of the sweet, late-winter work that once steamed here. While maple sugaring was not as prevalent here as areas east of Cleveland, it still provided much-needed, late-winter income.

Some homes on acquired land are historically significant; some homes are not. Then there is this French Creek Reservation home. Simply called the Bogdom home, this house shows both ingenuity and history. The rear of the home was actually a former interurban electric railcar. While this home stood as a sign of the rise and fall of the interurban, it, like the interurban, no longer exists.

Two

THE LADIES AND GENTLEMEN OF VISION

Henry L. Minert walks out of his new Ranger Office, which was anything but new. Minert knew that he had inherited the donation of a fantastic piece of property and this old house. In order to turn this former farm into a real metro park, he would have to hire staff, acquire equipment, and make alterations and additions to the land—and he would have to do so with very little money.

If one person could be credited with starting the Lorain County Metro Parks, it would have to be Richard W. McGinnis. Born in Youngstown, McGinnis grew up in the shadow of Mill Creek Park, Ohio's oldest park district. Thus McGinnis became quite accustomed to all of the benefits of green space, including the fact that parkland and services were essential to all aspects of healthy and thriving communities. He arrived in Lorain County in the mid-1950s as the new director of regional planning. Within months, he formed the Park Study Committee. This group quickly determined the county's interest in, and need for, a county park district, and they organized civic groups and local governments to petition probate court judge Harold S. Ewing to act upon the request for a park system. In just 16 months, McGinnis's dream of a Lorain County Metro Park District became a reality. The library at the French Creek Nature Center (FCNC) is named in his memory.

Judge Ewing had the pleasure of declaring, by means of journal entry of the probate court, the formation of the new Lorain County Metro Park District on May 6, 1957. While he fully agreed with the need for a park district, he knew that the ultimate responsibility of this new agency would fall upon his shoulders as judge of the probate court. To oversee the new metro parks, Ewing would have to appoint a governing board. As stated in the park district's *1959—1962 Progress Report*, "Judge Ewing exercised careful judgment in selecting a board of three Park Commissioners to serve without pay." Judge Ewing's solution to best represent all of the county's citizens was to appoint one commissioner from the northern, central, and southern areas of the county. On July 14, 1958, Judge Ewing swore in the first park board of J. B. Johnson, C. Leon Lehman, and Wallace J. Chapla. Ewing Hall at the FCNC is named in Judge Ewing's memory.

On top, the first board of park commissioners meets with probate court judge Harold S. Ewing in 1958. The lack of a director at the table suggests that this may have been the park district's first park board meeting. Per Ohio Revised Code 1545, the probate court judge appoints park board members to three-year, rotational, and unpaid terms. The gentlemen pictured here are, from left to right, C. Leon Lehman, Judge Ewing, Wallace J. Chapla, and J. B. Johnson. Below, Chapla served the park district as a board member for more than 21 years, more than any other park commissioner. This first board certainly had strict orders—to hire a director. This daunting task required a national search and involved some 60 interviews. In November 1959, the park board hired the Lorain County Metro Parks' first employee, director Henry L. Minert.

SCALE 1"=100'

MADE BY THE LORA'
N PARK DISTRICT [
ES DEPARTMENT OF
SURVEY DATA MAP

On November 16, 1959, landscape architect Henry L. Minert started his amazing career as the director/secretary of the Lorain County Metro Park District. It took him less than eight months to prove his worth. On July 1, 1960, Minert opened the first Lorain County Metro Parks Reservation —Mill Hollow. Minert quickly became well known for stretching the budget and organizing volunteer assistance and in-kind help. The park district's *1959 – 1962 Progress Report* states, in words possibly written by Minert himself, "The Director was not too proud to beg and scrounge used materials." His requirement to reuse nails and to build picnic tables out of used utility cable spools is not only legendary but ultimately genius. Minert would serve the citizens of Lorain County in this position for an incredible 23 years. The courtyard adjoining the lobby of the CVC is named in his honor.

She went by many names. When strung together her signature read Grace Annie Dorothy Bacon DeMuth. She was the last heir of the Bacon family estate, which was located within a spot in the Vermilion River valley known as Mill Hollow. Impressed with the plans of the new metro parks, DeMuth donated 110 acres to the park district. Within eight months, her former homestead opened as the first metro park.

Capt. Jabez Burrell built a majestic home in Sheffield in 1820. His grand homestead would make its mark in history, including a stint in the 1830s as Oberlin College's Sheffield Manual Labor Institute and as a notable stop along the Underground Railroad. For over 100 years, the Burrell family has held an annual family reunion; this one took place in the 1950s. The land donation by the family anchored the French Creek Reservation.

Three

WHEN THE PARKS WERE A PARK

It was classic Minert—free and functional. This was one of the first picnic tables in the first metro park, Mill Hollow. The table itself was made from a large utility cable spool. The stationary seats were from recycled telephone poles with planks nailed on top. This odd, and very fun, table withstood eight years of dedicated use until the river consumed it in a fit of flooding in 1967.

Lorain County Metro Parks' first director, Henry L. Minert (left), and an unidentified individual share a quiet moment. The Vermilion River's shale cliff dwarfs both of them and in doing so adds symbolic background to Minert's challenge; how can he possibly turn a family farm into a metro park and do it with hardly any staff, very little time, only a stipend of a budget, and towering expectations? Minert pulled it off by utilizing creative frugality, employing a few but very highly motivated staff and volunteers, and by hiring landscape architect and planning consultant M. Stephen Warner. In Warner's opinion, phases needed to be implemented; instead of developing the entire 110 acres of Mill Hollow, efforts were to be concentrated on one small section at a time. Minert used this approach and opened the first section of Mill Hollow one year before expected.

The majority of the Bacon farm was out-of-production farmland. With some grading and drainage, this land could easily be transformed into open space, play areas, and park roadways, but it completely lacked the shady scenery that park visitors would expect. It also would need picnic shelters and tables. All of this would be easy if the park district had money, staff, and equipment. They did, however, have Henry Minert.

The Vermilion River valley was Robert Hartle's childhood backyard. He knew every rock, tree, and deep pool of the river. How natural it was, then, for him to pursue a job protecting, enhancing, and sharing the land he loved. Starting as a foreman/ranger, he advanced to park manager, and then to operations supervisor. He even worked for several months as interim director. Hartle retired after an amazing 39-year career.

Hartle positions a post that will support the first traditional shelter for Mill Hollow. In his long career with the metro parks, Hartle saw many things come and go, including the old nature center, the Trading Post, and the wishing well. This appropriately named shelter, Shelter No. 1, came and stayed. It was ready for picnickers on Labor Day in 1960 and is still in service today.

Even today, this geodesic shelter would look modern. This one, however, actually greeted the first visitors to the first park in 1960. Its bargain price of $400 was erased by the fact that it required assembly. Original park employee Robert Hartle stated that it was one of the toughest challenges of his career. It did shade uncountable family picnics until a severe storm washed it away in 1969.

Five 12-by-16-foot summer cottage homes were donated to the Lorain County Metro Parks in 1960. Three of these were turned into small picnic shelters, like the one shown here. One was turned into the park's first version of a nature center. The last one was turned into an information center, and although long closed, it greeted visitors to Mill Hollow's "B" side well into the 1990s.

Henry Minert had such a knack of motivating help that he even called in the army. In this case, it was Company A of the 308th Army Reserve Battalion. The reservists, in turn, used this opportunity as a training exercise. Their major task was to clear small areas, cut trails, and build small footbridges.

This image shows the signing of the first camping permit on July 1, 1960. Boy Scout Troop No. 336 had the honor of being the first to spend a night in the new metro park. Seen here are scout master Don Grills (left) and the Lorain County Metro Parks' Harold Olds (right). For the first two years of the park, the camping area was just open space. Scout campouts were popular back then.

The addition of 12 family camping sites in 1962 showed just how popular camping was in the valley. Adjoining the campground, a large campfire council ring was added along with a large picnic shelter. The pond in the foreground was great for bluegill fishing and feeding the park's eclectic collection of ducks, but it was not used for swimming.

Camping became such a popular activity at Mill Hollow that a camping show took place in 1964. At the show, campers and visitors alike could check out the latest and greatest camping equipment.

As it still is today, picnicking was the main activity for visitors to the first park. Even though the utility cable spool table served visitors well, standard picnic tables were needed, and soon added.

The beauty of the cliffs was matched by the sheer pleasure of splashing and exploring in the clean, shallow waters of the river itself. Fishing was great, but crawdad hunting was undoubtedly more popular. Crayfish abound in the rocky streambed, and many instinctively backed into waiting nets, coffee cans, or brave hands. The flat nature of Cleveland shale certainly lent itself to many great skipping contests.

Turning farmland into parkland meant giving Mother Nature a hand. In essence, sunny farm fields had to be turned into shady parklands. In this 1962 image, an unidentified metro parks ranger is assisted in the planting of a spruce tree. From 1962 to 1963, some 800 trees and shrubs were added to the park.

Two pit toilet units arrived on the scene in 1961. While it is hard to complimentarily list the attributes of these primitive facilities, it must be assumed that they were undoubtedly an extremely welcome amenity to the first park visitors. Surprisingly they were not replaced until the late 1990s, when water lines came into the valley and allowed for flushing.

The historic home of Benjamin Bacon would serve many purposes in its history. Forthcoming would be its honor as the metro park's Mill Hollow House Museum. While this grand old structure was intact, it would require much in the way of modern upgrades, including a central heating system, in order to become suitable for public visits. Outside stands a carved version of the park mascot at the time, Ranger Andy.

Robert Hartle (left) and an unidentified helper repair the Mill Hollow House's parlor fireplace. In the hearth, they left one brick without mortar. This one, as history or tradition has it, was heated by the fire and then taken to bed as a warming brick. The truth to this is muddled, however, because some believed that the fireplace was not functional, but just decorative.

This view of the Mill Hollow House Museum shows the Mill Room. Today such a room would likely be called a home office. While it might take a bit of imagination to picture Benjamin Bacon sitting at this desk, the ledger book that sits on top of it is a mid-1800s original.

The chicken coop arrives. Adelbert "Bud" Novotny backs in a donated decommissioned chicken coop to Mill Hollow. How could Henry Minert have seen any use in such a donation? Surprisingly his vision on this project did not go far beyond the fact that this structure once held animals. As he saw it, it would again host animals, but this time wild animals as the Mill Hollow Nature Center.

The chicken coop is shown completed. Minert took the donation of a chicken coop and turned it into the Mill Hollow Nature Center. The coop sat on top of a foundation that was set into the hillside. The top of the structure held nature displays. The bottom was open space for programming and meetings. This cool coop served the Lorain County Metro Parks for some 30 years.

The inside of the Mill Hollow Nature Center held a wide variety of nature displays. Most of them described the plants, animals, and natural processes of the Vermilion River valley. Some, like this one, did their best to promote the interpretive services of the park district. All of the exhibits were constructed by staff using such tedious methods as real "cut and paste," stenciled lettering, and lots of construction paper.

While the Mill Hollow Nature Center held various live animals such as fish, frogs, and snakes, it was this unique honeybee hive that captured the attention of most visitors. Made from a hollowed-out slab of a tree trunk, this hive contained one frame, which made finding the real queen bee relatively easy. A tube to the outside allowed the bees to harvest pollen and nectar from the park.

On June 1, 1962, Perry Frank Johnson joined the executive staff of the Lorain County Metro Parks by becoming the park district's first naturalist. While his experience was in recreational programming, nature was his passion. His natural history knowledge and his amazing recall of the plants and animals was unprecedented. Johnson also brought the additional talents of photography and publishing. For nearly two decades, he single-handedly produced the park district's *Arrowhead* newsletter.

Johnson, seen at left in the pith helmet, tells a group of Head Start students some of the finer life history points of the animals at Mill Hollow's North American Wildlife Exhibit in 1965. It can be stated with the utmost confidence that any questions that these students might have had did not stump Johnson.

One of the Bacon barns stayed on and became known as the Trading Post. A small office on the back side served as a ranger station. The larger section of this barn is shown here housing mowers and animal care equipment, but this portion of the building spent most of its service time offering visitors bottled water. For decades, this was the only drinking water site in the park.

The scenic wonders of Mill Hollow did not stop with the cliffs. Over the first few years of the park, many trails were constructed that would allow visitors to see the nature of this special valley. This is an early view of the Bacon Woods Trail on the park's "B" side. To many, this is still the best nature trail in the park district.

From day one, Mill Hollow was popular. In fact, local newspapers often listed the weekend attendance figures. A busy weekend, however, left the park's trash cans full. Each Monday morning, the trash trailer would need to make its rounds. Notice the exceptionally high use of paper plates in this 1963 shot. These unidentified employees are seen passing a standard picnic table and heading toward a cable spool one (ahead left).

With the growth of the park, all aspects of park maintenance grew. Not only did grass have to be mowed and trash collected, but vehicles to do such tasks had to be acquired, housed, and maintained. Yet it would not be until 1978 that this maintenance facility would be added. Besides the garage and work space, there were also staff offices and a small garden where the staff grew vegetables.

The slope on "B" side was a natural sledding hill from the start. The shape of the hill allowed for all levels of sledding and climbing. During some years, lights would be added to allow for sledding during early evenings. These sledders seem to be having speedy fun, but they were going too fast for the photograph to show exactly what kind of device brought them down the hill.

Wintertime brings with it many additional opportunities to enjoy the nature of Mill Hollow. Water constantly percolates out of the cracks in the Cleveland shale and in winter freezes into amazingly giant icicles. Many park visitors make it a priority to see this frigid, but beautiful, natural event. This group, though, is distracted by a fairly common, warm weather park activity, a baptism.

Four

THE VISION GROWS

It was a 70-year-old house that sat at 126 Second Street in downtown Elyria, and it was scheduled for demolition. What could Henry Minert have seen in this home? On January 1, 1960, he opened it as the park district's headquarters. Now the park district had an address and a place to conduct all of its administrative business, and it would do so here for the next 21 years.

Metro parks fill many of society's niches. But wilderness search and rescue in Lorain County? While unlikely, this awesome vehicle was at the ready in 1972. It could go down the road, off the road, and over the water to handle everything from serious personal injuries to the fighting of forest fires. It is still not clear if it was ever used.

The Jackson home became the Black River Reservation's Jackson Nature Center. The notation on this 1965 photograph states, "wrecked by vandals immediately." This notation does not clarify if this meant the sign or the Jackson Nature Center itself. Since no images of the house as a nature center are in the metro parks' collection, then perhaps the mystery solves itself.

This 1968 image states, "Chambers pasture." To the eye of visionary park director Henry Minert, however, this was prime parkland and the perfect site for a day-use area of the new Black River Reservation. It was soon to contain park roads, parking lots, a shelter, and trails. Its name would be Bur Oak, after the giant trees that bordered its east side (right).

Chief naturalist Perry F. Johnson took this picture in 1969 by balancing on the railroad trestle that crossed the Black River in Sheffield. It shows a view north into the Black River valley, toward the city of Lorain. Johnson scoured the county with his camera looking for potential parkland. Did he see today's Bridgeway Trail weaving back and forth across the river in this view?

Black River Reservation's High Meadows opened in the summer of 1963. This park area featured several shelters, a pit toilet, and an eternally memorable playground. Henry Minert (left) cuts while ranger Chuck Warren (center) holds the ribbon. Seated at right is the Honorable Harold S. Ewing, judge of the probate court. The future of this park area would find it adjoining acres of retail stores.

It was called Astro City, and it was the coolest playground this side of Cape Canaveral. This rocket-themed structure contained an out-of-this-world collection of slides, ladders, ramps, and steps, all of which were supported by candy-striped legs. It was the most fun a kid could have, at least while on earth. Astro City launched its last astronaut in 1986.

The French Creek is the largest and northernmost tributary of the Black River. In Sheffield, it is joined by Jungbluth Ditch (also known as Sugar Creek) and Fish Creek. These small streams, and the woodland they flowed through, caught the eye of Jabez Burrell. In 1815, he saw this land as the perfect place to settle. In the 1960s, Henry Minert saw it as the perfect place for another metro park reservation.

It was the bed of the short-lived Lake Erie and Pittsburg Railroad spur. Once an impressive trestle spanned French Creek, but times quickly changed, and the trestle and rails were removed. However, the bed left behind was perfect for a scenic park roadway. Today most of the entrance road at the French Creek Reservation's Pine Tree Picnic Area sits upon this former railroad.

Until 1990, all of French Creek Reservation's activity was to be found at the Pine Tree Picnic Area. The entrance to this park area was off French Creek Road. This 1971 image shows a very atypical entrance sign. Also different were the design of the entrance roadway and the position of the park's gates. Still the same today, this area can be entered without actually going into the park.

His name was Edward Fulton, but everyone called him "Dewey." He was a career marine with a rock-solid handshake before becoming a ranger. Using his frugal ingenuity, he fabricated nearly all of the French Creek Reservation's original bridges, stairways, and guardrails. Note the odd combination of chainsaw and reading glasses in this image. The glasses were not likely for reading construction plans, of which he probably had none.

The project was called Lake Carlisle Reservation. It was going to put Lorain County Metro Parks on the map. Despite this claim, some saw it as a boondoggle; others saw it as a broken promise. Structurally and environmentally, it was questionable. Needless to say, it was the most controversial plan ever proposed by the Lorain County Metro Parks. When full, an 800-acre lake would have resulted. With the water would come an impressive collection of active and passive recreational opportunities. The hinge pin was an inflatable dam. New and basically untested, it remained to be seen if it would really work. This dam would be asked to hold back the muddy waters of the Black River West Branch. Even if it did work, holding back muddy waters in an agricultural setting had produced turbid and lifeless lakes elsewhere. The Lake Carlisle Reservation project never happened. If it were not for the fact that this project was a 1969 levy promise, it might have gone forgotten. Yet today, it still comes up in conversation.

Many of the parcels that went together to form the giant Carlisle Reservation had old homes on them. Some of these were razed, and some were renovated and rented. This one was turned into the Outdoor Education Center. The lower floor of this large block home hosted hundreds of programs from the mid-1960s through 1980. This image clearly shows that the long drive passed through some prime wetland.

Some of the most diverse, and beautiful, trails branched out from the Outdoor Education Center. Scattered among this bottomland area are dozens of woodland ponds that reflect both the surrounding forest and the many former paths of the Black River West Branch. In the 1980s, U.S. 20 routed right through the Outdoor Education Center and cut off access to this interesting area.

46

In July 1981, the metro parks had a new address. No longer would the administration work out of the old house on Second Street, but out of the new Carlisle Visitor and Administrative Center. The other half of the building was public space with one medium room, one large room, and even flushing toilets. For the first time, the metro parks could host programs in large, comfortable spaces.

The CVC was great for programming, but ironically offered little for the public to actually visit. In 1984, the addition of the Wildlife Observation Area (WOA) solved this problem. The award-winning WOA featured bird feeders and wildlife landscaping on the outside. Inside visitors enjoyed the wildlife through special glass and a custom sound system. The room also contained displays and the first Friends of Metro Parks Nature Nook Gift Shop.

The Duck Pond Picnic Area was a popular addition to the Carlisle Reservation. It provided two large, well-stocked ponds, a large picnic shelter, and uncountable ducks. The origin of the ducks was always suspicious, and feeding them was eventually discouraged for health reasons. As an aside, the name of this day-use area came from the natural ponds (actually old river channels), which are in the nearby valley.

As the name plainly states, the Equestrian Center was built for horses. Almost three miles of riding trails circle an arena and judge's stand. Summer weekends find the area filled with the excitement of horse shows and competitions. The horse trails lack stables, so riders are required to trailer in their own horses. Whether on horseback or "hoofing" it on foot, the gravel trails offer a great nature experience to all who traverse them.

In 1969, Otto Schoepfle arranged for the transfer of his incredible formal garden to the Lorain County Metro Parks upon his death. While not regularly opened to the public, Schoepfle (in the foreground with white shirt) did occasional tours. Here he leads the East Elyria Kiwanis Club in 1970. Each plant in the garden had a unique story, and it was a very special treat to hear about them from Schoepfle himself.

This small cottage, deemed Lodestone Lodge, sat along a sharp bend in the Black River East Branch in Grafton. This 1963 photograph shows clearly that it was built from the broken bits of sandstone that were left from the quarrying operation that once prospered there. Sadly the structure fell into disrepair, and around the opening of the surrounding Indian Hollow Reservation in 1975, the cottage was leveled.

Much of the land that was to become the Indian Hollow Reservation was treeless farmland. So volunteer groups, like these Boy Scouts, were employed to plant countless trees. But Indian Hollow Reservation also employed a different and quite slower approach to growing trees. Simply put, signs stating "reforestation" were erected to keep mower blades away and the public lightly informed. After 30 years though, these areas are wonderfully and naturally forested.

The clear and shallow channel of the Black River East Branch flows through the Indian Hollow Reservation over a solid bed of sandstone. While this sandstone was seen as an important and quite noticeable natural resource, the park's unusual plants go rather unnoticed. A very short list would include two-flowered Cynthia, rattlesnake-plantain, sweetflag, and giant cucumber magnolia trees. A rare and extremely unusual animal would be the freshwater jellyfish.

This one did not make it. The sandstone exposed at the Indian Hollow Reservation was perfect for making grindstones. Starting in 1860, the Grafton Quarry Company quarried out the sandstone and then rounded it into six-foot grindstones before shipping. All metro park reservations have taken a part of their unique nature and incorporated it within the park district's arrowhead logo. Naturally a grindstone is the featured image for Indian Hollow Reservation.

While other metro park districts around the state had ventured into new, and less traditional, forms of recreation, the Lorain County Metro Parks did not make this leap until 1975. That year the well-known Forest Hills Golf Course became the Lorain County Metro Parks' first active recreation venue, and the first one actually designed to generate revenue. The overall challenge, though, was to retain quality while keeping the greens fees low.

Ranger Tim Mahar strikes a pose next to the entrance sign of the oddly named Caley/National Wildlife Woods Wellington Creek Reservation. In a very roundabout way, the name comes from the will of the land donor, John Caley, and the original managing agency, the National Wildlife Federation (NWF). Amid much fanfare, the park officially opened on July 1, 1976. Note the embedded NWF logo just off of Mahar's right shoulder.

Originally the Caley/National Wildlife Woods Wellington Creek Reservation had a pond and a marsh. The pond was near the park's entrance, while the marsh was adventurously secluded. To reach the marsh, a crossing of Wellington Creek was required. To the joy (and sometimes dismay) of many hikers, that crossing was over this rope bridge. Here Ron Gariss (lower left) and Chuck Warren add the finishing cables. For safety, this bridge was replaced in 2004, sans cables.

The southern end of Lorain County rolls due to the sheer number of small streams. Most of these have their origins along the nearby line that separates Lake Erie's watershed from that of the Ohio River. A drive along New London-Eastern Road will reveal this rolling landscape and, as in this 1967 picture, pass the Funk Farm and the land that was to become the Charlemont Reservation.

Charlemont Reservation was unique throughout the state in that it allowed for the seasonal hunting of eastern cottontail (rabbit) and ring-necked pheasant. Lacking trails, most hunters and adventurous hikers would wander through forest and fields and eventually onto the Ramsey Road—an abandoned railroad that provided the most open passage through this unimproved park. Summer field-nesting birds, winter raptors, and a large yellow millipede highlight the park's wildlife.

When Carl L. Crapo came to the metro parks from the Lorain County Sheriff's Office, he brought with him a wealth of talent and new energy. His easy leadership persona meshed perfectly with his willingness to join in. His work as the metro park's first deputy director led him on to becoming the second director of the park district in 1982. Here Crapo (right) shares some time at the county fair.

For the 1986 levy campaign, metro parks director Crapo promised the citizens that the metro parks would bring services and facilities closer to the population center of the county. The levy passed, and Crapo fulfilled this promise with the FCNC. This nautilus-shaped structure, which looks surreal in this aerial photograph, featured large program areas, a deck, a library, a gift shop, and a permanent display area.

The permanent display area of the FCNC featured natural history museum–styled exhibits that reflected the nature of the forested 428-acre French Creek Reservation. The exhibits mixed stylish permanent structures with changeable interactive displays that addressed the collective interest of "streakers, strollers, and studiers." Sound stations, matching challenges, touch-screen computer games, and this flowing ravine all allowed these displays to fulfill their function.

Carl Crapo was able to secure outside funding to construct an eight-acre lake at the Caley/National Wildlife Woods Wellington Creek Reservation. While the funds were flowing, the water was not. The lake was built in the summer of 1988, and Lorain County experienced its hottest, and driest, summer on record. Needless to say, the lake did not fill very quickly. To the right of the image is Caley's pond, and to the upper left is its marsh.

The house that Benjamin Bacon built got its just reward in the 1980s, when it was officially placed on the National Register of Historic Places. Here operations supervisor Robert Hartle (left) is joined by planner Ron Twining (right). Everyone was well dressed for this special occasion, except the house itself. A new siding of yellow poplar had just been completed, and an exhaustive study into the home's original colors was underway.

Five

WILDLIFE AND
WILD WEATHER

It is hard to separate wildlife from the role of a metro park. Whether injured or orphaned, on display or used in programs, or encountered along park trails, wildlife and metro parks were partners. When Mill Hollow opened in 1960, it became clear that wildlife would be a part of this new park system. While the parks protected wildlife within its borders, the public and the park district wished to show off wildlife in a more convenient setting. Within a year of the opening of Mill Hollow, animal cages started to appear, and the beginnings of the park's North American Live Animal Exhibit had begun. Wildlife continued to be a part of the park district's image well into the 1980s. But as laws changed, and staff expertise swayed, wildlife became less of an apparent part of the Lorain County Metro Parks' work and most wild animal displays highlighted fish, frogs, and snakes. In the early 1990s, however, wildlife programming and displays came back home to the park district with the opening of the Carlisle Raptor Center. This literary raccoon would, no doubt, approve.

In 1962, the park district opened the North American Live Animal Exhibit. Located in the former farm field behind the Bacon House, this collection of animals delighted visitors for years. As the name suggests, however, the animals in this dynamic collection were not always wild. Ducks, sheep, and other farm animals brought about the sense of a petting farm to the exhibit.

Park ranger/wildlife manager Larry Wickham does his best to control triplet white-tailed fawns in this 1964 photograph. In a "Name the Fawns" contest, these three kids were donned Domino, Tag-a-long, and Ranger. While the positive media of these fawns was great, captive breeding was not the preferred means of maintaining the captive herd.

This 1962 image shows the capture of one of the North American Live Animal Exhibit's most notorious residents, Buck. Somehow Buck wandered into Bagley's Packinghouse Market in downtown Lorain. Dazed and confused, he was cornered in the basement. To the rescue came the Lorain County Metro Parks' Larry Wickham (left, holding deer) and Bob Murphy (right, holding deer). Buck would spend his remaining days at Mill Hollow wreaking similar havoc.

According to wildlife officials, the wild deer population in Ohio is higher than it has ever been. This still does not squelch the joy for most people when they see these magnificent animals in the wild. The excitement of seeing a fawn in an animal enclosure fades when compared to spotting one like this along a quiet stretch of trail.

Wildlife enclosures were mostly gone from the metro parks in the late 1970s and 1980s. In the early 1990s, they returned with great excitement as the Carlisle Raptor Center opened. Featuring hawks and owls, this collection has been highlighted by the addition of a bald eagle in 2003 and this peregrine falcon in 2005. Named Havoc, this bird came only a short distance to become a resident of the raptor center. Hatched from an egg under a bridge in nearby Rocky River in 2004, Havoc enjoyed only two months of flying. In July of that year, he permanently injured his right wing. The metro parks' staff and volunteers have worked with Havoc, and in 2007, he should be trained and ready for programming. And at that time, he, like the other residents of the raptor center, will become an impeccable ambassador of raptors, wildlife, and nature.

Lorain County Metro Parks manages the land in order to manage the wildlife. When proper habitat is maintained, special things can happen. The mitigated wetland restoration at Sandy Ridge Reservation caught the liking of this sandhill crane pair in 2001. This endangered species has nested in this park ever since. This particularly bright bird is apparently reading up on the virtues of the wetlands mitigation process.

The Lorain County Metro Parks was honored to display this 12,000-year-old woolly mammoth skeleton at the CVC in 2005. Unearthed in Siberia, this is one of the most complete skeletons on display anywhere. Like many of the Lorain County Metro Park displays, this special exhibit had no fee associated with it. It was such an impressive sight that it even attracted the interest of former chief naturalist Perry Johnson.

Many big trees call the metro parks home. None raise as much debate as this one, however. Growing at the north end of the Black River Reservation, this massive eastern cottonwood owns a circumference of over 20 feet. Its upwardly bent branches suggest that it might be an Indian signal tree. Its relatively young age, however, suggests otherwise. Still it shares the arrowhead logo on this park's entrance signs.

Despite its appearance, this giant sycamore tree is living, and growing well, in the middle of the Vermilion River Reservation's Bacon Woods. Gaping hollows are a normal signature of sycamores, but this view does not show the loving carvings that cover this tree's back side. In a statement of its health and endurance, this hollow tree withstood the full fury of the 1992 tornado without any harm.

Many native wildflowers, including these Virginia bluebells, grow well in the rich soils of many of the Lorain County Metro Parks reservations. Considering that most of the county's original forest was removed by settlers, and the land subsequently farmed, it is surprising that any native plants remain. Reduced to tiny, protected pockets or stored in dormant seeds, many plants did survive and are once again allowed to thrive on park district land.

Spring brings warmth, rain, and sunshine to the floor of the forest. This erases the grays and tans of late winter with an explosion of color in the form of spring wildflowers. With the cabin fever season over, thousands of visitors flock to the Lorain County Metro Parks reservations to enjoy the fulfillment of nature's promise of regrowth. Putting an exclamation point on this season is the state's wildflower, the white trillium.

From high on the Vermilion River's cliff, Perry Johnson took this tranquil picture of Mill Hollow on May 30, 1969. Notice the campers in the foreground, the animal cages and string of parked cars in the center, and the Bacon Museum just above center. It is an idyllic, and very typical, weekend scene for the park. Did anyone know what was to come in five week's time?

On July 4, 1969, an unprecedented storm dumped some 13 inches of rain in less than 12 hours on the area. The resulting flood set a new standard for what was believed to be the definition of a century flood. As viewed from the cliff the day after, the floodwaters had already receded some. Still the valley was fully covered by the Vermilion River and by unparalleled devastation.

At the height of the July 4, 1969, flood, the Vermilion River had covered the roadway of the North Ridge Road Bridge. As seen in this image, the river sweeps just under the bridge's decking. It is important to note that the normal level of the river is some 25 feet below this bridge.

Mill Hollow's North American Live Animal Exhibit is viewed several days after the July 4, 1969, flood. Did the animals even have a chance? While the screening of the right-hand cage filtered the rushing water, the one on the left took a direct hit from a log and toppled on its back side. At the peak of the flood, the rushing water would have topped the rooflines of these cages.

In most winters, the water seeping out of the Vermilion River's shale cliff paints the scene with thousands of icicles. If the freeze lasts long enough, these frozen structures can grow to gigantic proportions. The largest icicles in this image measure nearly 90 feet from top to bottom and dwarf these fashionably clad hikers.

Generally Cleveland's west side receives only a fraction of the snow that the east side's "snowbelt" gets. This was not the case in the winter of 1977–1978. Heavy snow persisted throughout the winter, and snowplowing became one of the major tasks of the park staff. In this image, park planner Rich Harmych (right) takes his turn at the wheel while an unidentified employee musters up a wave.

Extended periods of freezing weather can cause the surface of the placid Vermilion River to freeze nearly solid. This makes for an image of amazing beauty. However, it can spell disaster if the deep freeze is followed by a stint of unseasonably warm weather. The frozen surface will crack into angular pieces of ice that pile together to form an ice jam flood. The Vermilion River is noted for such floods.

This great image shows the Vermilion River, as seen from the North Ridge Road Bridge, during an ice jam flood in 1982. While the river seems to be flowing well here, the water level is well past flood stage for the park, thus indicating that an ice jam has formed downstream. While uncommonly used today, dynamite was once the cure for ice jams.

To the least extent, ice jam floods inundate the park with floodwater. If rain is part of the melting weather, then the flooding can become quite excessive. The high water level closes the park by shutting off roadways and trails. Perhaps this image of Mill Hollow's Shale Cliff Trail could still be accessible by canoe.

To the greatest extent, ice jam floods float enormous chunks of ice at breakneck speed. In this case, it was break-toilet speed. The damage to this pit toilet at Mill Hollow shows the immense damage that these floods can cause. Besides the repair to the building, the ice chunks themselves can be extremely difficult to move. If the meltdown is followed by cold weather, then the chunks just lay around.

As extraordinary as the flood of July 4, 1969, was the tornado of July 12, 1992. This Sunday afternoon twister tore down the west wall of the Vermilion River valley and then bounced around haphazardly until it climbed up the east cliff and headed off east. Where once there was a solid wall of trees, this day-after image shows the selective cutting the tornado did to the Bacon Woods.

The devastation of the 1992 tornado at Mill Hollow is hard to capture on film. This image, however, does the damage some justice. Where once large trees stood together, this shot shows the extent in which they were toppled and torn. To further add breadth to the image, note how the scene proportionally shrinks the hiker on the right.

These three trees show the indelible signature of the 1992 Mill Hollow tornado. The sounds and smells of the next morning mixed with the visual destruction to create a powerful memory that defined this example of nature's power. The county would suffer two more consecutive days of tornados. During this outbreak, no serious damage happened to any of the park district's structures.

This is one of the most curious images in the Lorain County Metro Parks' photograph archives. The back of this 1965 image, taken at the Black River Reservation, simply states, "Burned area. Cause—meteor?" While no physical meteor is to be found in the "Metro Parks Meteor Collection," it does create a very clever euphemism for describing the most likely source of the fire—that being the misdirected energy of youth.

Six

SERVICES AND FACILITIES

"Fire in the hole!" The Union army gives a live demonstration of the Civil War's heavy artillery, sans cannonball, at Mill Hollow's Pioneer Days in 1988. This annual festival, which will celebrate its 30th year in 2007, typifies the detail, diversity, and dedication that the Lorain County Metro Parks puts into its programming. While the park district started in 1957, it could be said that the promotional presentations that took place before then, the ones designed to spur interest in starting the parks, were actually the first Requested Programs. Published Public Programs came a little later. While nature hikes and traveling slide shows dominated the offerings for more than half of the Lorain County Metro Parks' history, the expansion of public interest did not just coincidentally mirror the expansion of park district facilities. Whether through programs, structures, or just increased public relations, it has always been the first job of the Lorain County Metro Parks to ever improve its ability to serve its collective bosses—the citizens of Lorain County.

Ranger/park naturalist Perry F. Johnson, second from the left, ushers them off and leads them out. Starting in 1962, Johnson solidified the park district's call to conduct professional educational programs. His amazing knowledge of nature touched uncountable students, scouts, and families, and he set the standard for all the staff that followed him down the trail.

A nature hike in the metro parks is the epitome of a field trip. These Lorain City school students look as if they know what is coming, not the content, perhaps, but the excitement and adventure that happens when a nature expert leads them off into the wilderness. Until recent cutbacks in school funding resulted in less field trips, such programs were the emphasis of the naturalist department. Still today, such programs are free.

Busses have played various roles in the programming service of the metro parks. While most carried people, this bus carried the park district itself. Named the Parkmobile, this bus served as a mobile nature center. Visitors found exhibits within on plants, animals, and even astronomy, along with park district promotional pieces. Rumor has it that this bus actually ran so poorly that it was typically towed to visitation sites.

In the 1970s, the Lorain County Metro Parks initiated a unique program called Senior Bus Trips. Simply described, a park district–owned bus would take senior organizations on tours of Lorain County with emphasis on the metro parks. In the 1990s, a second bus, with a chair lift and VCR monitors, was added. Part-time staffer Carolyn Walker has headed up this program for most of its existence with graciousness and corny jokes.

Junior Naturalists was the king of all summer camp programs. Starting in 1974, this weeklong program took upper elementary students through a fun, and fairly intense, nature workout. The highlight might have been the Friday night awards ceremony. Shown here, Gary Hawke (standing right) gives out a certificate to an unidentified "Junior Nat" while (left to right) Beth Fetterman, Lyn Modic, and director Henry Minert show approval.

It would be hard to imagine ranger/ naturalist Roy C. Hartman not holding a snake, or some other type of wild animal. For over 30 years, he expressed his obvious, and infectious, love for wildlife and public service. Certainly no other naturalist did more programming for the metro parks than "Ranger Roy." Hartman's love for raptors, maple sugaring, and trains changed the face of the CVC campus.

Before the construction of the CVC, most of the programs conducted by the naturalist department were nature hikes. With consideration to weather and school calendars, most of the hikes were squeezed into the month of May. Here naturalist Gary Hawke (hand in air) leads a class of students on a late spring hike through the French Creek Reservation in 1974.

Certainly no other form of wildlife commands more interest and, as this picture clearly shows, attention than birds of prey. Obtaining state and federal permits, along with the expertise for caring for these special birds, is difficult but well worth the work. Here naturalist Gary S. Gerrone, or more correctly, a red-tailed hawk, captures the attention of the campers during an outdoor program in 1985.

Naturalist Kelly Bauer is blurred by the steam of the evaporator in this 2003 maple sugar program. These students have already tapped a tree, taken a train to a sugar bush, and learned that real maple syrup is actually boiled down tree sap. Here in the sugar shack, they not only get to see the sap evaporated into syrup, but they get to taste some as well.

Naturalist/park manager Tim Fairweather leads a discussion on the Wonders of Wetlands at the Johnson Wetland Center at the Sandy Ridge Reservation. Smaller centers became the norm during the 1990s. Structures at Sandy Ridge, Mill Hollow, Amherst, and Schoepfle Garden hold less than 100 people, but do so with attractive flexibility. These small rooms are extremely popular as public rentals as well.

Nature programming themes were stretched in the 1970s. In this craft program, participants learn how to make a pinecone wreath. Other similar programs evolved to the point where the nature of the program became more based upon the interest of the public. This 1976 shot shows unidentified participants working within the former confines of the Carlisle Reservation's Outdoor Education Center.

Volunteer Deanna Walther (left) leads a group of other first-person interpreters and visitors in a Christmas carol during the park district's unique Pioneer Holiday program. Staged in the Bacon Museum, this program is much like walking through an ongoing play. Visitors are welcome to interact, but the impressive knowledge of the cast does not go beyond 1865. Three historic structures have initiated an increase of history programs.

The Klondike Derby was a popular Boy Scout challenge during the 1960s and early 1970s. Organized by the Scouts, the metro parks basically served as a host for this program. Few outside organizations have consistently used the metro parks as a host for their programs. Certainly the most notable exception is Operation Open Heart. Lorain County Law Enforcement agencies have conducted this program at Mill Hollow for 44 consecutive years.

Cross-country skiing has had an ironically up-and-down history with the metro parks. In the 1970s and 1980s, occasional lessons were offered and well received. In the 1980s, Friday Night Ski Hikes would happen, if there was snow. A late 1980s donation caused an expansion of this program and even a dedicated room for free rentals at the FCNC. Still the consistent lack of snow doomed this potentially popular program.

The Forest Hills Golf Course is one of the best examples of the expansion of programming opportunities in light of the ever-changing interests of the public. While far from the nature of classic metro parks programming, golf courses offer the public a chance for healthy outdoor recreation. For this reason, Lorain County Metro Parks is hardly unique among Ohio park districts with golf courses.

SplashZone came upon the metro parks under the radar. The park board thought it best not to simply accept this incredible donation from philanthropist Eric Nord, but to do a little study first. A survey by Lorain County Community College tallied a 92 percent public approval for this project. Considering that seven percent of the population typically does not swim, SplashZone seemed to be a great direction for the park district to go.

The Lorain County Metro Parks has, almost from the start, taken its mission on the road. This image shows an incredibly detailed relief map of the Vermilion River Reservation as displayed at the Lorain County Fair in 1962. The park district still annually participates in the Lorain County Fair, but other venues over the years have included most community festivals and several stints at the local mall.

The Lorain County Metro Parks has taken a wide variety of programs and displays to the local Midway Mall over the years. Some have been tied to themes such as Earth Day or law enforcement. Others have taken temporarily vacant stores and filled them with grand exhibits with live plants and animals. In this 1992 mall exhibit, naturalist Lisa Novak, standing near the center, gives a quick, hands-on lesson on spinning.

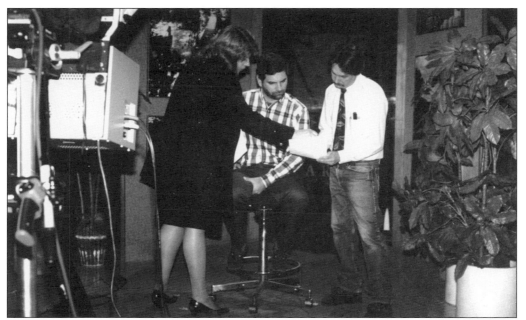

A Place in the Parks was a local cable television show produced by the Lorain County Metro Parks and Lorain County Community College (LCCC). The show balanced time between in-studio guests and in-the-field segments. Here the Lorain County Metro Parks' Becky Voit (left) confirms directions with LCCC director John Quissenbury (right), as Lorain County Metro Parks' host Gary S. Gerrone (center) looks on.

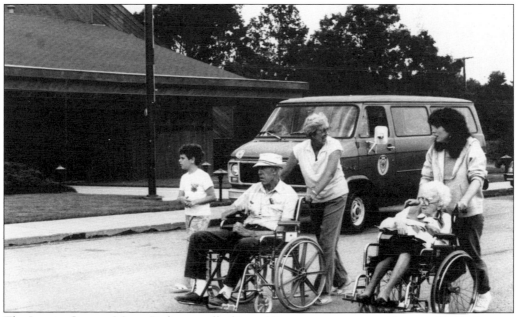

The Lorain County Metro Parks tags all of its public announcements with a nondiscriminatory statement. While the rough and rugged wildness of metro park lands would seem to lend itself poorly to persons with physical challenges, the park district's services and facilities fall closer to the other end of the spectrum. All park facilities are handicapped accessible, and most trails are gravel or paved and have gentle inclines.

The Friends of Metro Parks is a nonprofit organization that assists the park district in uncountable ways. While this organization offers a wide variety of benefits for its members, it is this group's volunteers who take center stage. Hundreds of volunteers put in tens of thousands of hours for the metro parks each year. This expertise and total hours equates to the hiring of several full-time employees.

The Friends of Metro Parks conducts many annual fund-raising programs each year for the benefit of the park district. They also maintain several ongoing programs. One of the best known is the operation of the Nature Nook Gift Shops. Currently located at the Schoepfle Garden Visitor Center, the CVC, and the FCNC (shown), these stores allow visitors to purchase everything from a butterfly field guide to a plush dinosaur.

Ranger Andy appeared in various forms as a mascot for the Lorain County Metro Parks from the early 1960s until the early 1980s. E. E. Davidson of Wellington carved an early version of Ranger Andy using a chainsaw (see image on page 31). That version differed significantly from the cartoon drawing shown here (by Huiett). This "Andy" version contains aspects that suggest he is still made of wood.

With Ranger Andy's retirement in the early 1980s, the Friends of Metro Parks assisted the park district with the creation of a new mascot. Thinking that a predator would be inappropriate, an herbivorous chipmunk was chosen. To give the public some input, a naming contest was held. The winner was Chip E. Munk. "Chippy" served the park district for some 15 years but has gone into semiretirement.

A less noticeable service of the park district is that of natural resource management. Proper care of the land results in healthier populations of plants and animals. Sometimes the management program is quite intensive, like this prescribed burn. The results of this apparently destructive practice is impressively apparent within weeks, as new, healthy, and preferred plants sprout forth from the charred earth.

Often resource management makes more obvious sense. These nesting boxes, over water, are for wood ducks. However, wood ducks seldom use these boxes, preferring to nest in tall hollow trees in woodlands. Does this mean that the metro parks needs to grow tall, hollow trees? Certainly, but in the meantime, tree swallows, or maybe an eastern screech-owl, might happily take up residence in one of these boxes.

While many programs of the park district show success through local statistics and praise, it is hard to know how the Lorain County Metro Parks stands up to other similar agencies. Awards, both local and national, have been bestowed upon the Lorain County Metro Parks over the years as a testament of the high level of program quality. Here director Henry L. Minert (left) accepts the 1972 National Associations of Counties Achievement Award.

Metro parks' commissioners Andrew Foreman (left) and Dorothy Shriver (right) surround director Carl L. Crapo as the threesome shows off a set of awards from the Great Lakes Training Institute in Indiana. The Daniel L. Flaherty Award went to the park district's new and innovative Wildlife Observation Area in 1985.

Metro parks' public services supervisor Christie L. Vargo (right) awards Perry F. Johnson the (then) Association of Interpretive Naturalist's Pioneer Award in 1983. One aspect of Johnson's career that was notable in his receiving of this award was the massive and well-organized photographic library that he managed. Many of his images, especially from the early years of the park district, appear in this book.

Pioneer Days is a weekend time machine that takes visitors back to the days when modern conveniences might have included a sharp ax, a wood-burning stove, and an excess supply of flour that could be used for barter. This festival has been attracting tens of thousands of people during the weekend after Labor Day for almost 30 years. Showing great authenticity, this blacksmith brought his whole shop.

Halloween Fair started out as an educational scout program that told of the myths, legends, and truths of Halloween. Through the years it has evolved, changed locations, and grown to three weekends in October. A spooky train highlights one area of the program. Refreshments and games highlight another. It is the haunted forest trail, however, that still steals the show. Here the iconic Pumpkin Lagoon stares back at the camera.

In 2002, the Short Loop Trail that circles through the woodland behind the CVC was electrified. As promised, a holiday lighting program was started. Now in its fifth year, Holiday Lights has become one of the most unique holiday lighting programs in the area. Featuring a drive-through portion, the *Holiday Express* train, and a sponsored trail filled with themed stations, this year-end program attracts thousands of visitors.

While this image seems to have been taken in the early 1800s, it was not; nor was it taken outside. This amazing picture shows the level of authenticity of the 2003 Ohio Bicentennial Exhibit. Staged in Ewing Hall at the FCNC, this major exhibit was a partnered celebration between the park district and historic organizations in Lorain County that highlighted Lorain County's unique contributions to Ohio's history.

Annual major exhibits have become synonymous with the Lorain County Metro Parks. These displays immerse visitors into some exotic location or distant time, using live plants, animals, and impressive scenic features that give these exhibits a full sense of realism and permanence. Each of these displays has several "wows." This ice age exhibit featured an impressive collection of animatronic animals including this woolly mammoth. The admission fee of $1 is now legendary.

To improve the ability of the metro parks to serve the public, the park district developed a computerized reservation system nicknamed "RES." RES allows visitors to schedule a nature hike, reserve a shelter, and to pay for a SplashZone membership, all with one call. RES works so well that several park districts across the state have approvingly copied RES. The public can access portions of RES through the Lorain County Metro Parks Web site.

Stan Pijor (left) has touched many lives over the years. While most might consider his years presiding over Lorain National Bank to be his most successful, he is likely to disagree and softly state that his years as a member of the Lorain County Metro Parks' board of park commissioners were much more rewarding. For all that he has done for the greater Lorain County community, and for the metro parks, Lorain National Bank sponsored the fabrication, equipment, and maintenance of the unprecedented Stanley G. Pijor Distance Learning Classroom at the FCNC. While this special facility is a great classroom, it presents itself as a movie theater. Seating up to 100 people, it comfortably hosts movies, along with lectures and entertainment-based programming. But that is only a small portion of this room's capabilities. Through cameras, monitors, and a computerized hookup, the Lorain County Metro Parks' staff can beam educational programming to classrooms, museums, and nature centers throughout the world. Additionally global venues can broadcast live, and fully interactive, programming into the distance learning classroom; it is like taking a trip without leaving home. Here Pijor receives a permanent reminder of his special classroom from reining probate court judge Frank J. Horvath.

Seven

THE NEW PARKS

In 1993, Black River Reservation was a popular park, but it had not changed much since it opened almost 20 years before. It still contained gravel roadways, pit toilets, a tangle of muddy trails, and little hope for expansion. The 1950 Bottom Land Park Plan (page 14) had dreamed of a park that stretched further north. The majority of this additional land was owned by the City of Lorain. Previous discussions had taken place, but not until the early 1990s did some real possibilities surface. Lorain mayor Alex Olejko entered into deliberations with the park board, including commissioner Stanley G. Pijor and interim director Bob Hartle. Then James Daniel Martin, only the third director in the park district's history, finalized the offer. The park district agreed to take on the land and to add at least $200,000 worth of improvements to the property. A few million dollars later, the "new" Black River Reservation was born. The old section of the park was also renovated and connected to the new by the remarkable trail bridge shown here.

Many metro parks in Ohio are known for their scenic roadways. While the new Black River Reservation seemed to lend itself well for a parkway, new director Dan Martin thought differently. With community approval, construction of the Bridgeway Trail began. This paved trail would erase the land's abused areas, enhance its amazing scenery, and become the most visited trail in the park district.

Metro park's director Dan Martin (left) hosts the first of his many park openings and rededications—this one at the Black River's new Day's Dam in 1994. Metro parks' commissioner Stanley G. Pijor (second from left) grew up in this valley, thus making him an official "River Rat." Also pictured is Lorain mayor Alex Olejko (standing) and Lorain County Metro Parks' commissioner Sherrill "Cookie" M. McLoda (far right).

The Black River Bridgeway Trail is quite true to its name. It bridges together the two most populated communities in the county, Lorain and Elyria. It bridges people with nature. It bridges the Black River three times and does so with just two bridges. And it bridges the remarkable beauty of the park with all people. This tram allows those needing a little extra help to enjoy this beautiful park.

The newer section of the Black River Reservation was neglected for years. Impact on the land by various legal and illegal misuses made it seem highly improbable that it could ever become a metro park. But nature heals itself well, and the regrowth of some of the areas was not less than miraculous. The Thirty-sixth Street Ditch Falls shown here was once the dumping ground of trash, including whole cars.

By the mid-1990s, the Vermilion River Reservation, still fondly known as Mill Hollow, needed some TLC. But how does one renovate the flagship of the park district? Carefully, and with flush toilets! The Carriage Barn, shown here, was dedicated on June 22, 1996. Not one nail supports the frame of this true post-and-beam structure, which was built new to look old. A large barn room inside supports programs and public activities.

The chicken coop that became the Mill Hollow Nature Center (see page 33) had gracefully outlived its usefulness. In 1996, it was torn down to make way for the Mill Hollow Amphitheater. This open-air venue is home to the Lorain County Metro Parks' Summer Concert Series, which hosts an average of 300 people on summer Sunday nights.

The first trailhead signs contained simple maps that allowed visitors to get lost more comfortably. Many of these were replaced over the years with clearer, more detailed, and much more accurate maps. Then there is the Mill Hollow Walking Center. This trailhead allows for hiker orientation, park natural history information, and benches for quiet contemplation. This mid-1990s image shows that the forest beyond has greatly filled in since the 1992 tornado.

The Vermilion River Reservation started with 110 donated acres. A decade later, it contained some 600 acres. In the 1990s, director Dan Martin and the park board were able to increase this park's size past 1,000 acres. Most of this new land centered on the Vermilion River corridor and included this important parcel known as Chance Creek. A keen eye will notice the Peasley Road Bridge near this image's center.

The nature, scenic beauty, and even hunting at the Charlemont Reservation were enhanced through a grant from the United States Department of Agriculture. This program added nearly 20 small wetlands that greatly increased the park's natural diversity. The management of various grasslands at the Charlemont Reservation has resulted in increased birdlife, including nesting sparrows and winter raptors.

Since its opening, the Charlemont Reservation lacked trails. This park also did not allow for horses. In the late 1990s, these two situations partnered to greatly improve this park. The Lorain County chapter of the Ohio Horse Council gained approval from the park board to cut and maintain equestrian trails in the park. Now horseback riders and hikers can access this great park on trails such as this one.

The parking areas of Indian Hollow Reservation's Sheldon Woods are across the river from the majority of this park's land. In the 1990s, a multifaceted improvement project was completed to solve this situation. The hump-backed bridge shown here allows hikers to enjoy the improved Beech-Maple Trail. In 1992, Indian Hollow also opened its nonimproved trails for mountain biking. Through careful stewardship, this popular activity has not shown any significant negative impact.

Through the assistance of the Village of Grafton, the Beech-Maple Trail at Indian Hollow Reservation became the first with an official community connector trailhead. While hardly scenic, this trailhead fully allows the citizens of Grafton to access their hometown metro park without having to drive around to the park's entrance outside of the village limits. This successful idea was also incorporated into the construction plans for Amherst Beaver Creek Reservation (ABC).

For much of the last 15 years, improvement projects have annually taken place at Forest Hills Golf Course. While most holes received new tee boxes, the entire course benefited from the construction of a reservoir and a computerized watering system. Also, the awkward original entrance road and parking lot were reconfigured and paved, and this large gazebo was added overlooking the front lake.

Forest Hills Golf Course has long been known as one of the most scenic public golf courses around. Besides this, the cost to take on the course's 18 challenging holes has always been considered modest. A multiyear cart path–paving program added a great sense of country club to this course in the 1990s, and annual landscaping upgrades have enhanced the course's natural beauty as shown here.

Sandy Ridge Reservation opened in 1999, and with it came many new levels of park district stewardship. A large portion of this park's funding came from outside the budget and included grants, donations, and money from the wetlands mitigation process. The Johnson Wetland Center, shown here, is an environmentally green building. However, the managed habitats of Sandy Ridge Reservation are better known and offer the best wildlife viewing in northern Ohio.

Sandy Ridge Reservation's ability to host an incredibly wide variety of wildlife is the direct result of the quality of its major habitats. Over 320 acres of field, forest, and wetlands share the park almost equally. Sadly, few visitors wander the Meadow Trail, but everyone must head down the Wet Woods Trail to get to the sought-after wetland. In this image, birders check out a woodland sighting.

The wetland mitigation process provided the funding for the restoration of Sandy Ridge Reservation's wetland. Various agencies assisted the park district to ensure that this project would not end up as just a water-filled hole. The shallow water, the impressive seed bank, and the introduction of lost native plants have made Sandy Ridge Reservation a living success. Here

a great egret poses near the observation mound. Endangered species such as bald eagle, sandhill crane, and American bittern have nested in this park. The overall diversity of birds at Sandy Ridge Reservation has made it a top birding site in Ohio and beyond.

Seen here is the room with three lives. The Permanent Display Room at the FCNC served the public very well for nearly a decade, but as often is the case, the displays grew tired and old and failed to catch visitors' imaginations. In an unprecedented move, the exhibits were replaced with an indoor playground. Named Displayground, this room perfectly mixed recreation with education. For this room's third life, see page 90.

Within the nautilus shape of the FCNC was an original color scheme that emphasized red, blue, and yellow against the building's white stucco and gray block walls. To make the contrast even greater, most of the building's floors were alternate black-and-white tiles. Certainly the 2004 renovation to earth-toned floors, full wall murals, and a rushing ravine turned this eclectic building into a pleasing nature center.

From the start, the step-down area in FCNC's lobby was called the Kiva. Slightly more functional than attractive, the Kiva served many duties for both staff and visitors. The 2004 renovation, though, took the usefulness of the Kiva to new levels; actually, fewer levels would be more accurate, as fewer, wider, steps allow for chairs and benches. The fireplace and art gallery are also new additions.

Originally called the Multi-purpose Room, this large space at the CVC once claimed an unreasonably high stage and a flame-orange back wall. The recent renovation added wood paneling, walls full of timeline-themed exhibits, a cozy seating area with a fireplace, and a new name—Black River Room. Narrower and lighter tables allow this room to fit the needs of both naturalists and visitors.

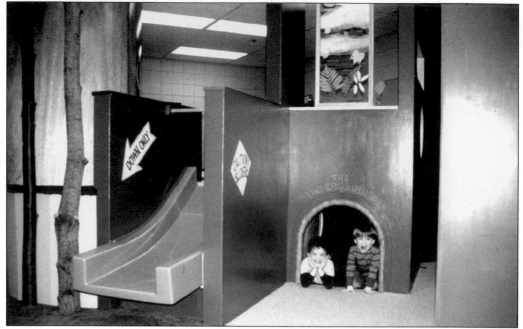

To better serve the public's ever-changing needs, some of the public and staff rooms at the CVC have traded places. This room was originally called the Classroom. Back then it possessed a "school lab" look. In 1996, it became the Children's Nature Space. Cleverly layering space, kids could now learn about nature while crawling, climbing, and sliding. As seen here, it opened with a habitat theme. Today dinosaurs rule.

The cedar exterior of the CVC always gave false a impression of the building's interior. Being mostly block and tile, the inside motif was strongly utilitarian. In the early 21st century, a renovation gave the building the wealth and warmth of wood mixed with earth tones. A large hallway gallery, with a custom hanging system, gives visitors monthly changes of décor and local artists a chance to show their wares.

The grounds of the CVC's campus features many fun and impressive attractions. No doubt, the most popular is the Carlisle Raptor Center. This display facility houses birds of prey in a close-up, open-air setting. Much of the funding for the various phases of this facility came from generous donations. While some may have given more funding, none touched the hearts of the staff, visitors, or birds more than a Wellington preschool that raised over $1,000 by running sponsored laps around the outside of their school building. In 2006, an adopt-a-raptor program began with an initial response that more than insures both the success of this program and the continued professional care of the birds. The facility itself features many of the common raptors of the area, along with the state endangered barn owl, bald eagle, and peregrine falcon (see page 60). Most of the raptors are also "trained to the fist" and make appearances for both Public and Requested programs.

The Carlisle and Black River Railroad might be the hardest-working train in the county. It services fun at many programs, including the maple sugaring run shown here. The custom engine was sponsored by the Friends of Metro Parks. Roy Hartman, naturalist and engineer, designed and laid the track and did much of the programming. The engine's name, *Old No. 6*, is in honor of Hartman's former unit number.

The Nielsen Observatory presents itself like something out of this world, and that is pretty close to what it is. It came about through the passion of gifted amateur astronomer Dr. John Nielsen and his wife, Rose. After Dr. Nielsen's passing, his incredible telescopes needed a new home. Through unprecedented donations, and ongoing assistance from the Black River Astronomical Society, the Calisle Reservation's Nielsen Observatory was born.

Before his death in 1992, Otto Schoepfle was able to give his stamp of approval on the many improvements that were being planned for his "garden that grew." One necessary improvement was to create a visitor center. The opportunity to do this presented itself in the 1990s in the form of converting a neighboring home. This carriage house structure now hosts a gift shop, meeting room, deck, staff offices, and flush toilets.

Sadly more people came to know Schoepfle after his death because access to his magnificent gardens became greater. Most people assumed that the grounds would be little more than a large backyard with extensive landscaping. The expression of sheer surprise and joy of first-time visitors to this formal arboretum, however, is nothing short of endearing. This image shows a variety of hostas and ferns in the shade garden section.

Snow covers the "schlag" topiary, giving it the whipped cream look that it is trimmed to imitate. Otto Schoepfle's garden was greatly influenced by the gardens that he visited in Europe. This shrub—taxus actually—represented the whipped topping that commonly tops many hot desserts and beverages in Germany. The popularity of the schlag is well shown as many neighbors of this park mimic it within their landscapes.

The North Coast Inland Trail (NCIT) is the longest and skinniest park in the district, and it sets its paved surface upon the bed of the old Toledo, Norwalk, and Cleveland Railroad. Open to all forms of foot traffic and nonmotorized vehicles, the 13-mile-long Lorain County portion of this trail will someday pave its way to Toledo and beyond.

"B 219" is not a Bingo call. It is actually the distance to Buffalo. A few of the old railroad markers were left along the NCIT. Unfortunately, the trail does not go east past Elyria—at least not yet. The marker stating that it is 321 miles to Chicago is much more applicable. Through partners, the NCIT will, in the near future, stretch that far west.

The long and skinny nature of the NCIT would seem to lend itself to little diversity, but this is not at all the case. The trail passes through forests, fields, and wetlands, as well as cities, farms, and villages like Kipton pictured here. The funding for this Rails to Trails project came mostly from the federal government and not from the Lorain County Metro Parks' capital budget.

The City of Amherst, like most communities, wanted a metro park within its borders. The ever-rising cost of land, plus the Lorain County Metro Parks' commitment to other projects seemed to make this impossible. But by combining the resources of the city, metro parks, and individuals, groups, and businesses from the community, the ABC became a reality. This building is a near twin to the one at Sandy Ridge Reservation.

For many years, the Lorain County Metro Parks' facilities were only available for staff programs or for the use of nonprofit organizations. In the late 1990s, the park board decided to allow for a fee-based rental system for all groups and activities. While other park buildings might be larger, no other facility hosts more groups than this one at ABC.

Tall pines form a cathedral-like setting over the highland portion of the paved trail at ABC. This rolling trail crosses the namesake Beaver Creek twice, and extends a community connector branch east to a nearby neighborhood. While this portion of ABC measures only 65 acres, the trail winds over one mile, and through surprisingly diverse habitats and great scenery.

Beaver Creek is the largest completely inclusive watershed in Lorain County. The stream flows north through South Amherst before reaching the park and before flowing a mile and a half further north to Lake Erie. A century ago, a working trail paralleled the creek. Called the Pony Trail, this path allowed mules, and gravity, to carry the large blocks of quarried sandstone to waiting ships on Lake Erie.

Eric Nord, left with suit and no hard hat, always wanted to sponsor a "year-round, multi-generational, aquatics facility." On Memorial Day weekend 2002, his wish came true with the opening of SplashZone. Here Nord and his wife, Jane (right of Nord), listen to Lorain County Metro Parks' director Dan Martin (right with back to camera) outline this impressive project during the groundbreaking ceremony. Commissioner Sherrill "Cookie" McLoda is seated adjacent to the left of Martin.

Nord sponsored one-half of the cost of SplashZone. The other half came from individuals, businesses, and the City of Oberlin, SplashZone's hosting city. None of the construction cost came from the metro parks. The facility features both indoor and outdoor pools, plus weight-lifting and workout rooms. A classroom area not only allows for instruction, but serves very well for birthday parties.

Since its opening in 2002, SplashZone's outside pool was dominated by a 168-foot-long water slide. Certainly not out of loneliness, a second giant slide was added in 2006. When not sliding, outdoor bathers can splash in the soaking pool, get splashed by the dunk buckets, or play on the in-pool playground. An impressive dry-land playground is also a major attraction.

The outdoor pool at SplashZone features an in-pool playground that has fun piled upon fun. In the shallows, children can have soaking fun with dunk buckets, a mushroom shower, a water slide, water cannons, and various showering pipes. This exciting feature is within a pool area that features a safe and shallow sloping entry called "zero depth." This means that there is no pool lip to trip over.

This great frog is spitting out a child at the "tot pool" inside SplashZone. This special pool keeps the fun going as children can splash and slide within an enclosed portion of the indoor pool area. Besides sliding, toddlers can play basketball or chase the sprays of water from the surrounding water jets. The custom wall mural was painted by former Lorain County Metro Parks employee David Wenzel.

The main indoor pool at SplashZone features an eight-lane competition pool. This pool is also fun for splashing, exercise, and swim lessons, along with high school swim meets. Two one-meter boards were joined by this fun array of slides in 2004 (shown here). This pool's size also makes it a great place for other aquatic activities such as kayak lessons.

Columbia Reservation opened its trails in August 2003. This represented another park area purchased and opened as per the 1961 Proposed Park Reservations plan. While the forefathers may have known well that this area was important to the park district and the county's citizens, they may not have foreseen that the entire park would be purchased and developed through the Wetlands Mitigation process and not through Lorain County Metro Parks' budget.

Columbia Reservation not only hosts the Rocky River West Branch, but many acres of reclaimed wetlands. These wetlands vary greatly in nature, and this diversity allows for many different occurrences of plants and animals. For example, beavers are common in this park, and they work hard to alter these wetlands. On the flip side, two rare birds, the glossy ibis and the little blue heron, have been spotted in this park.

Lakeview Park came into the fold on July 4, 2006. This special lakefront area marked the 24th metro park area. Lakeview Park has long been an iconic lakefront park owned and operated by the City of Lorain. The city called upon the reputation of the Lorain County Metro Parks to bring this special park back to its former glory. Nearly all of the funding for this project came through donations.

This old postcard shows the former glory of the Lakeview Park Rose Garden. It was a garden filled with thousands of well-kept roses, within an equally well-kept setting. Over the years, the upkeep of this area faded, and so did the blooms. In 2006, the last few roses were removed, the beds and walkways were completely redone, and an irrigation system was added. Lastly, 1,248 sponsored roses were planted.

The Lakeview Park Rose Garden started to take shape in the early spring of 2006. The first phase of planting resulted in 1,248 individual rose bushes being installed. Studies and public input gave the park district the ability to reintroduce the same roses that had originally graced this garden. Every rose, and some whole beds, were sponsored in honor or memory of friends or families.

The Lakeview Park Rose Garden project started in late winter of 2006 and opened on July 4. It was an exhausting dream come true. Here the board of park commissioners relaxes in the opening moment with Lorain County Metro Parks director and philanthropist Robert Campana; included here are, from left to right, Campana, commissioner "Cookie" McLoda, commissioner Stanley G. Pijor, commissioner Kirk E. Stewart, and Lorain County Metro Parks director James Daniel Martin.

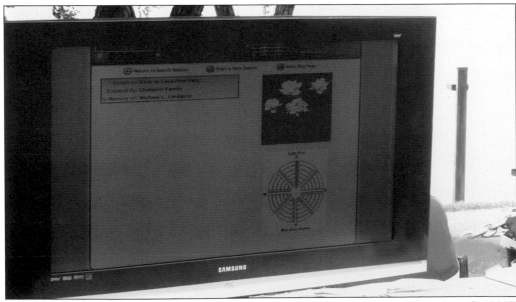

The rose garden represents just the beginning of Lakeview Park's improvements. In 2007, more sponsored roses will be planted and a new bathhouse will rise up from the 1917 original foundation. Improvements to beachfront amenities will also take place. This image shows the computer-generated program that will allow sponsors to find their rose and allow everyone to read the touching stories behind each sponsorship.

Wellington Reservation was a collaborative between the Lorain County Metro Parks and the Village of Wellington. The result was an incredible 550-acre metro park reservation that is second to none. The entrance at the north end of the park passes near the 21-acre Wellington South Reservoir. This lake not only makes for great reflections, but it also makes for great recreation.

The interior of the Wellington Reservation Visitor Center is unusual in that it is a two-story structure. The upper story, accessible from stairs or an elevator, contains a loft gallery and an observation deck. The main floor, shown here from the loft, contains plenty of open space, a great fireplace, and a large wall of windows that overlook the Wellington South Reservoir.

The Wellington South Reservoir once supplied water to the village and adjoining areas of southern Lorain County. Because of increased demand, a much larger reservoir was built across the street, leaving the south's waters much quieter. Here a canoe plies the still water of the Wellington South Reservoir. However, the metro parks' pontoon paddleboats, which will be free to rent, will likely make a huge splash in the summer.

The Wellington South Reservoir is not the only water in the Wellington Reservation. Several hundred acres of the park have been restored as wetlands through the wetlands mitigation process. This shot shows a typical scene where grassland meets wetland. The combination of these two habitats will greatly enhance this park's ability to host nesting grassland birds, migrant and nesting water birds, and wintering birds of prey.

Eight

THE FUTURE

Since the 1961 Proposed Park Reservations Plan, the Lorain County Metro Parks has systematically moved toward reaching each area and community of the county with parkland, along with the award-winning services and facilities that have become synonymous with the park district. To achieve this monumental task, it has been necessary for the Lorain County Metro Parks to keep abreast of the wants and needs of the community, and to be able to adjust and adapt to ongoing changes and challenges. While some specific plans and activities need to be promised, and drawn up, the main plan should always be for the Lorain County Metro Parks to be more proactive than reactive. All plans need to include land purchases, but many of these will undoubtedly come in nontraditional forms. The moonscape shown here might tell this story best. In 2007, a trail leading north out of the Black River Reservation's Day's Dam area will traverse the slag field of the Lorain steel mill and bisect the nature of the Black River and the history of the Burrell homestead.

The Lorain County Metro Parks would seem to have migrated up the Black River to East Thirty-first Street and to a dead end. Thus the increasing energy and activity of the Lorain Harbor area could never be connected to that of the metro parks, at least not without a boat. Vision along with collaboration, however, sees this differently. In 2007, a trail will pass north of Day's Dam and into the slag fields of the steel mill. This would not seem to be a place for a metro parks trail, but it is. This is the steel mill that built Lorain. It is a part of its history. While the trail will pass near desolation, it will also pass the current channel of the Black River. The Black River has been drafted into all of this development, but it has always remained true to its natural roots. What could be a better lesson, in nature and history, than to walk the ridge between the two? Certainly, this is a great place for a metro park.

Is this a place for a metro park trail? In 2007, a trail will push forth through this man-made wilderness and toward the Lorain Harbor area. The snow of this image certainly enhances the lack of life on the slag piles. The Black River, though, seems to carve a soft channel through it all. This bleak area is near where the first sightings of the county's return of the beaver and bald eagle occurred.

This was the 1917 Lakeview Park bathhouse. Looking stately and solid, it met its fate at the hands of the 1924 tornado. All subsequent structures have failed to capture the feeling of the original building. In an effort to return Lakeview Park to its original grandeur, the Lorain County Metro Parks has designed a new bathhouse that will capture the essence of the original, yet provide today's park users with all new amenities.

While Ohio park districts usually stay within their namesake counties, hardly any of them do. Lorain County Metro Parks is no different. It was in 1969 when Otto Schoepfle granted his incredible Erie County garden to the Lorain County Metro Parks. Since that time, the park district has focused on issues within the county borders. In the 1990s, however, the work on the NCIT began in earnest. This Rails to Trails project had many local advantages, but many distant issues too. While the Lorain County Metro Parks would build and maintain the local trail, the abandoned Toledo, Norwalk, and Cleveland rail line extended west far past the county's border. Many governmental agencies and nonprofits were already in line to take on other out-of-county portions of this trail, except for a small section in Huron County. With Huron County having little funding or organization, the Lorain County Metro Parks was able to step in and secure a linking section of this great trail.

South of Jan van Wagner's Avon Lake street is a stand of trees that was undeveloped. She knew that saving this woodland would be almost impossible, but van Wagner liked the odds. Her Save the Woods committee provided the park district with 170 acres of undeveloped land. By working with the city and the metro parks, this area will open as a metro park reservation in the next few years.

"Buddy" Miller is a man of many talents. His hidden parcel of land in Avon shows off many of these skills, but all focus quickly turns to his amazing ability to grow things. His 1990s donation of land to the Lorain County Metro Parks seeded an ongoing program to solicit purchases and donations of adjacent land in order to form a future metro park reservation here.

While metro parks are well known for land purchases, and natural history programming, some of the emphasis of the future will undoubtedly be centered on preserving the county's history. Currently the park district owns, maintains, and programs three historic structures. Events such as playing a melodeon by lamplight must exist comfortably in the future.

The Lorain County Metro Parks is a national leader in implementing the wetlands mitigation process. Using this tool, the park district has obtained millions of dollars to purchase, build, and enhance many park projects. Columbia Reservation, for example, was funded completely outside of the park district's capital budget. The future certainly sees the metro parks continuing to be a frugal fiscal steward of the county's citizens' money.

While the current volunteers, staff, director, and board of park commissioners of the Lorain County Metro Parks would like to stay on for another 50 years, it will be the youth of today that will carry this torch. And what may seem to be just a natural curiosity on a dewy summer morning may, if properly encouraged, turn into a career of public service.

ACROSS AMERICA, PEOPLE ARE DISCOVERING SOMETHING WONDERFUL. *THEIR HERITAGE.*

Arcadia Publishing is the leading local history publisher in the United States. With more than 3,000 titles in print and hundreds of new titles released every year, Arcadia has extensive specialized experience chronicling the history of communities and celebrating America's hidden stories, bringing to life the people, places, and events from the past. To discover the history of other communities across the nation, please visit:

www.arcadiapublishing.com

Customized search tools allow you to find regional history books about the town where you grew up, the cities where your friends and family live, the town where your parents met, or even that retirement spot you've been dreaming about.